Rhymes
for the

End Time
Church

Vickie Bryan

Table of Contents

Part 1

Let the Church Arise

Jesus Gave His Life

Why must I toil in my mind at this time?
One look at the news gives me the blues.
I wonder, "where is the love sent from above?"
It is here, do not fear. God's church draws the lost near.
Rise and see that the harvest is here.
Do not listen to the sound of fear as the end draws near.
Satan holds the world through lies so they will die.
Do not hide the truth. We must regroup.
Get your eyes on the prize.
At Calvary, Jesus shed his blood on the cross and he did
it all for free.
It is a mystery, you see. Why would Jesus give his life for
you and me?
He did so we can be with him for eternity.

Church Arise in Faith

Jesus fulfills his word from the depths of eternity.
He laughs at the enemy.
Church arise in faith.
Do not forget we have a date,
to glorify the Father, who cannot wait.
It is love that draws the lost.
It is His power that transforms them,
from death to life, this is God's delight.

Reach the Lost

Hell on earth was Satan's plan.
God cannot stand the sin of man.
In Genesis 6, the fix was in.
Nephilim mindsets filled the land with heartless men.
It grieved God's soul; this would have to go.
So, God sought a righteous man to birth his plan.
Noah built a boat so it could float.
Thus, beginning the plan for the birth of the son of man.
Now after the cross, look at the land.
It is full of sin once again.
Because of the cross, not all is lost.
God's church must arise to seize the plan,
to prepare for the return of the son of man.
It is time to reach the lost because of the cost paid on the cross.
In this hour, the power of awakening is released.
That God's love might free the lost from the devil's delusion
and bring them to the truth of his kingdom's solution.

Part 2

SalvationDrawsNear
Be Born Again

Hate Bait

Hate will bait you. It is a mistake that will take you on a
path that won't last.
Rage will arise as a disguise to take you to the grave
before your day.
Why take the bait?
Fall on your knees. Say pretty, please to the one who can
stop the stampede through the gate, to the fire, set by
the liar in the black attire.
You have a chance to say, "NO, I do not want to go."
Cry out to the one who came with his blood.
He will cleanse you from the hate that seeks to take you
to the fire set by the liar,
till you are filled with his love sent from above.
Then you can say, "Jesus freed me from sin. I have been
born again!"

Salvation Train

~⟵T⟶~

There is a fast train moving down the track.
This is the train of salvation for those who won't turn
back.
Get aboard this train provided by Jesus at Calvary.
The Father's plan frees from slavery to sin and death.
Our Messiah's life didn't cease by his test.
Three days later, he was free from the grave.
There is no need for you to die and be lost.
Why die when Jesus paid the cost?
Call out to Jesus. He will hear,

cleanse you of sins and dry all your tears.

Will You Take Me

Are you wise in your own eyes? On that day, what will you say? *"I never thought I'd have to pay."* *"I heard about the Lord who brings light, but I chose to ignore and didn't do right."* *"I also heard you were nice."*
"Will you take me anyway, even though I'm not right in your sight?"
But the Lord will say, *"I don't know you, so let me show you."* *"When you ignored my cross, you were lost."*
"Eternity with me was given for free, but now it's too late. You sealed your fate."
"Away from me, you will be for all eternity."

Ask Him

I am filled by my Father's love sent from above.
His love overflows my heart.
It is his love that saves,
heals and fills me.
Are you empty? You need his love too!
How do you get this love that flows from God?
Ask him. He sent his son Jesus to demonstrate his love.
Try it, do not hesitate.
Accept Jesus before it is too late.

Choose Life

Are you ready to meet your maker?
Do you want to evade the undertaker?
Choose life this night, become holy in his sight.
Jesus Christ gave his life so you would not perish in
your sins.
It's time to be born again and dwell deeply in him.

Be Born Again

I the Lord see the destruction of man upon the earth.
Violence is a curse that sin has disbursed.
Death and destruction always want more.
Run from sin,
'Let me in and be born again.

Escape the Fate

You all have a date with fate—a date you cannot escape. The gift of life will not last because of the sin of the past. It happened in the garden, where Adam and Eve were deceived. The command was given, "Don't eat from the tree; that would take you away from me." They ignored my word because of the devil's lies. Thus, humanity separated from me. How about you? Will you ignore me too? Will you accept the lie that you will not die?

There is an escape from the fate of eternal death. Jesus paid the price for sin on the cross. Three days later, he arose from the dead. Do not remain lost. Jesus already paid the cost.

Believe in Jesus. He made the way to escape the fate of the wide gate that would take you to hell. Will you ac-

cept my gift of eternal life? Will you change your mind and turn to me? So that you won't spend eternity with the liar that wants you in the fire. You need to turn, so you will not burn. I am waiting.

If you believe in your heart and make me your Savior, I will forgive your sins, and you can be born again. Here's how to pray. Call out and say, "Jesus, I am a sinner. I have done wrong." Please forgive me. Come into my heart and cleanse me so I can be with you and escape the fate of eternity without you. If you believe in your heart and declare with your mouth that I (Jesus) am your Lord and Savior, then, with me you'll be for all eternity.

Scriptures from the Bible

Jesus replied, "I tell you the truth, unless you are born again, you cannot see the Kingdom of God." John 3:3 New Living Translation (NLT)

---

11 Jesus ....' 12 Salvation is found in no one else, for there is no other name under heaven given to mankind by which we must be saved." Acts 4:11-12 New International Version (NIV)

---

16 For God so loved the world that he gave his one and only Son, that whoever believes in him shall not perish but have eternal life. 17 For God did not send his Son into the world to condemn the world, but to save the world through him. 18 Whoever believes in him is not condemned, but whoever does not believe stands condemned already because they have not believed in the name of God's one and only Son. John 3:16-18

---

9 If you declare with your mouth, "Jesus is Lord," and believe in your heart that God raised him from the dead, you will be saved. 10 For it is with your heart that you believe and are justified, and it is with your mouth that you profess your faith and are saved. Romans 10:9-10 NIV

If you would like to accept Jesus as your Lord and Savior, then it is your time to be born again.

Pray the following Prayer from your Heart.

Heavenly Father, I ask that you forgive me of all my sin.
I believe Jesus died on the cross to pay the penalty for
sin and arose from the grave three days later. I ask you
Jesus to come into my heart and be my Lord and Savior.
Thank you for forgiving, loving, and accepting me as a
child of God for all eternity

Name: _____

Date: _____

I am Born Again

I am clothed in Jesus Christ.
I am no longer clothed in sin.
I have been born again.
I have no fear of hell, can't you tell?
The glory of God rests upon me.
The blood of Jesus set me free.
I don't live in fear of dying.
I opened my heart and invited Jesus in.
He forgave me of all sin.
I am born again

Part 3

God is Good

Thank You

Father, thank you for your grace that stopped me from heading to the fiery lake. You sent your son to shed his blood on a cross for the lost.
Thank you, thank you, thank you!
For making me one with your son who shed his blood,
That I might be one with you too.

Jesus Set Me Free

I'm more than a conqueror, can't you see?
Jesus has indeed set me free.
He is my Lord and my king.
To him do I give glory and sing.

I Will Worship

The heavens declare your glory.
Creation tells your story.
How magnificent you are, the creator of the stars.
I will get on my knees and glorify thee.
I will worship the one who rescued me.

Fill Me with Your Presence

You are worthy of praise.
You are worthy of worship.
Holy Spirit, I adore you.
I implore you to fill me afresh and anew,
with your presence and the essence of your love.

Anointing

Holy Spirit I am thrilled that
I am filed with your Presence.
I'm excited because you are God Almighty.
Let your power flow to confirm your Word.
Stepping into your anointing is not disappointing.

Your Love

I Love you, Lord.
I love you, and I always will.
You fill me. You thrill me with your love.
Your love never tires. It never expires.
Your love is a continuous flow into my heart.
It has been present from the start.
I know your love for me will never part.

Holy Spirit

Holy Spirit, I love you. Holy Spirit, I adore you.
Your presence brings light and fills me with life.
It shakes me and breaks off what needs to go.
Then I can walk in a Holy Spirit overflow.
Flood me with your love raining from above.
I feel your presence, and I am filled with joy.
You are love and came to give me a big hug.

Power in the Name of Jesus

The name of Jesus is higher than any other name.
When we declare his name, we change the game.
His name contains the fullness of the power of God at
any hour.
It never falters, but it alters and brings release.
At the mention of his name, the enemy's actions must
cease.

Trinity

I believe in Jesus, the essence and presence of the Father.
There's no one higher, Father, Son, and Holy Spirit.
It is fair game to say they are one and the same.

Unity

~T~

There's no denying you are God.
People come from near and far to be in
your presence. It is your love that sets them free.
And the Father who binds us in love and unity.
One body, one mind as it is with the holy trinity.

Speak the Word

I feel pain in my heart when I see the news.
The world is filled with so many lies that I despise.
Still, the word of God can change all things.
He tells us to speak his word to release light into the
darkness.
That chaos and evil might flee and usher in God's
brightness.

Let the Glory Shine

May the glory of the Lord fall
upon the church for all to see.
The Lord has released tremendous power for this hour.
Do not be discouraged but encouraged!
Because he has set you free and given you liberty.
As the son of man walked upon the earth,
so shall his sons and daughters as well.
You are different from the sons
of the earth who are under a curse.
They are distressed, but you are blessed.
There's a test for your faith, so do your best.
Allow the glory of the Lord to shine upon you in these
end times.

Let it Flow

The glory of the Lord has risen upon us.
We are his children, called by his name.
Magnify the Lord in your coming and going.
Praise him, worship him with your life.
Here is a question from him to you.
Are you reflecting my glory?
Are you reflecting my peace, my patience, my joy?
I have more.
I will release an overflow that saturates every area of
your life.
It will flow from you to others.
Let it flow. Let it go.
For when you do, there will be even more from me to
you.

Grace and Favor

Grace set the pace for me. God gave it for free.
Grace releases favor so I can savor the goodness of my
Savior.
When I give a financial seed as God directs, I can expect
his favor.
Favor releases God's power at the right hour to bring a
financial shower.
And now I bask in abundance because the Lord is my
sustenance.

Signs, Wonders, and Miracles

Jesus heals today, and it will stay that way.
Signs, wonders, and miracles flow from the indwelling
Holy Spirit.
No room for us to boast.
Jesus walked this way. Why should we delay?
Signs, wonders, and miracles let them flow.
All you need to do is start, and God will do his part.

God is Near

Thank you for your power in this hour.
Don't live in fear; God is near.
Faith will overtake fear, so stay clear of its lies.
Find the truth in God's word and give fear the boot.

I Am

I Am and I have not changed.
My ways are the same.
My word is alive and will never die.
Believe the truth and reject all lies.
Resist sin.
Allow my glory to arise from within.

I am an Insider

Jehovah Jireh is my provider.

He is taking me higher.

I am an insider. I am born again.

Part 4

Truth

Abortion Kills

Abortion kills the baby inside. It's just cells they say.
Who could tell it's a baby anyway.
Deceived by lies the baby dies. The mother regrets she
believed the lies and her baby is not by her side.
Jesus knows your pain and regret; he offers you forgive-
ness.

Love of Money

Money, money, money is not my honey. This affair with
money cannot go on. I don't trust you anymore. You're
not showing up on time, I don't have a dime. What is
my crime? I work all the time. Have I made money my
master? This is a disaster. It must be, I lack prosperi-
ty. I've got to change and get my heart right. I will tithe
so my future will be bright.

Forgive

Oh the torment of my soul,
I have a grudge and I won't let go.
I was done wrong, my feelings are strong.
I did not deserve tobe treated that way.

What shall I do? Forgive them,you say. But they did me
wrong! My thoughts revolve,these feelings are strong!
How doIgo on?

Oh, I see, I am in prison bymy own decision. Now I
have a grudge by my own admission. Oh ok, my grudge
is sin. I must forgive when someone does me wrong.
This torment has gone on way too long.

Free at Last

You've been set free for victory.
You weren't made to live in fear; this is clear.
When you look and see my love on the cross and what
it cost,
Why should you not receive my liberty?
Here I am, Lord. Set me free from fear. Please draw
near.
I give you my pain as I look upon your cross.
You paid for my shame with your blood that stained.
I accept your gift of love.

I am free at last. You released me from my past.

Healing a Wounded Heart

Pain will stain your heart and set you apart.
Pain from a wounded heart can seize and freeze you.
I (Jesus) can heal and deliver from any wound.
Trust my love.
Draw close to me, and I will gently expose the devil's lies
so that you can thrive from the inside.
Healing is yours, and it shall endure.

You Never Leave Me

You are glorious, formidable, and full of power and
might.
You fill me with joy in your presence
and holy delight.
You are with me through the night.
I never leave your sight.

He Rescued Me

He rescued me from my mess.
Without him, my life would be in such distress.
I called out to him from my heart again.
He forgave my pride and stayed by my side.
I'm not the same. So much have I gained
from his mercy again and again.

The Curse is Broken

The curse has been broken. His blood has spoken.
I am set free from the curse of the law.
He hung on the tree for me.
So, all curses are broken.
His blood has spoken.

Help Me Discern

Thank you, Lord for your love sent from above.
It cures our woes on earth below.
Who am I that you are mindful of me?
From eternity you see all that concerns and bothers me.
Let me see as you see, that I might be free from my
woes.
Help me to discern. Thank you for your concern!

Trust is a Must

Trust is earned let us discern.
Jesus transforms our lives through the power of the
Holy Spirit.
He is trustworthy, kind, and faithful.
His love is good, holy, and stable.
He is able to fulfill his word for us.
Trusting him is a must. There is nothing to discuss.

Fear Must Go

Fear must go. Do not let it grow.
Fear is the opposite of faith.
It will steer you away from God's plan,
so you will not stand.
So please move with the grove of faith and keep your
destiny date.

Chaos

Chaos comes from darkness to
block the light released from God.
The light will overtake darkness
with the brightness of his glory.
And finally, that will put an end to the story.

A Prophet Who Deviates

A broken pair of scissors will not cut, so now what?
What good is a boat that cannot float?
A prophet that deviates from my word is absurd.
That one is not good for my use. What is their excuse?
What shall I do? Their divine purpose will not surface.
They exalted themselves above me, such loss at a high
cost.

Tragedy

Tragedy comes by the strategy of the enemy. Sin opens
the door for Satan to explore ways to destroy you.
Sin is a charmer, like a farmer always planting seeds.
There is no other way for you, but sins deeds.
Satan lies, he knows Jesus died to cleanse the guilt from
the inside.

Youth

If you're young, don't be dumb. Your youth will not
last, soon it will pass.
Is Satan pulling your strings? No, you say, "I'm just
doing life my way."
I'm young I can't be overcome.
When wisdom speaks, don't retreat, it will keep you
from defeat.

Old

I'm old, how can God use me? Remember, Moses
stepped into his call at eighty,
even when he told God maybe.
Don't choose me, "Let someone else say it please."
It was God's plan and Moses had to stand and fulfill
God's plan even at eighty.

Diamond

You were a diamond in the rough. Now you're being
buffed to reveal the depths of my glory.
Glory that sparkles with from within giving praise and
glory to him.
Life as Jesus paid for, life as Jesus was raised for.
Zoa life replaces death and decay with the glory that
raised Jesus from the grave.

True Prosperity

True prosperity comes from Jesus, out of our relation-
ship, you see.
I knew you before you were conceived.
I made plans for you, and I wrote them down.
Why be filled with fright when your life doesn't go
right?
I am the one who makes things right.
Does your plan look like mine?
It is time to reconsider.
Frustrated, discouraged, hopeless?
Those are not my gifts. Faith that endures is what you
will receive.
My word will endure any test, but you must rest in what
I say.

I am taking you through a brand-new way

Transform our Land

This is a dream that is picking up steam.
Come Lord, have your way without delay.
We give you the glory. We give you praise.
Take us by the hand. With you, we shall stand,
As you set out to transform our land.

Assault on My Land

A Word of the Lord on 6/5/20

This assault on my land, I cannot stand. I established this nation to give my people the liberty to worship me. This assault upon my land will not stand. I have given my man the plan, and my power will flow through him in this hour. I have given him a prophetic mantle, and he will begin to expose the darkness. The perpetrators of evil and wickedness will begin to brag about their atrocities and lies. In their pride, they will not survive. People will be judged by their words. They will give an account.

Stand up, America, for righteousness was given by me on Calvary. Do not think that I am not aware of the wicked. A righteous wave will flow, and my people will pray and seek me. I will turn this land around. I will set its destiny back on my established timeline, not the enemy's plan. But my enemy and his officers will be caught in their own trap.

Praise Jesus

The glory of the Lord has descended upon us.
We are his children, called by his name.
Magnify the Lord in your coming and going.
Praise him, worship him with your life.
Are you reflecting his glory?
Are you reflecting his peace, patience, and joy?
He can give more.
He will release an outpouring,
that saturates every area of your life.
It will flow from you to others.
Let it flow, let it go. For when you do,
there will be even more from him to you.

www.ingramcontent.com/pod-product-compliance
Lightning Source LLC
Chambersburg PA
CBHW060429050426
42449CB00009B/2208